For God's Sake

To Hannah.

Many, Many, thanks for
your help. this week.
you are a Gem.
love Helen
xxx

For God's Sake

SAL SOLO

daybreak

First published in 1993 by
Daybreak
Darton, Longman and Todd Ltd
1 Spencer Court
140–142 Wandsworth High Street
London SW18 4JJ

ISBN 0–232–52022–4

A catalogue record for this book is available
from the British Library

Scripture quotations are taken from the Jerusalem Bible, published and
copyright 1966, 1967 and 1968, by Darton, Longman and Todd Ltd and
Doubleday & Co Inc and used by permission of the publishers.

Cover: Leigh Hurlock

Phototypeset in 10/12 Souvenir Light by Intype, London
Printed and bound in Great Britain
at the University Press, Cambridge

Contents

Foreword

The first time I ever saw Sal Solo was on a Thursday night. I was sitting in my front room watching the TV and he was performing on *Top Of The Pops*! It was not until some years later that I was to have the privilege of meeting Sal face to face. By that time he was presenting a show for a radio station and I found myself being interviewed by him about 'Christmas Cracker', a new youth project that I was planning to launch that year. Talking to him I was surprised, excited, and, to be honest, at first a bit suspicious, when he told me that he had become a Christian.

The problem is that we live in a world where a lot of 'famous names' of one sort or the other, claim to be 'born-again' but then leave us wondering as we subsequently hear reports of their lifestyles, attitudes, opinions or statements which, with the best will in the world, sometimes appear to be in stark contrast to anything that Jesus ever did or taught about. I am pleased to endorse this collection of Sal's prayers and stories because I want you to know that over the years since our first meeting, I've slowly got to know Sal and know he is very different.

Some of my friends will want to remind me that Sal is a Roman Catholic and that I belong to a very different Christian tradition. My response is that I chose to write this foreword simply because Sal is a personal friend of mine whom I can honestly say reminds me of Jesus. In fact, he radiates a real sense of God's peace and Christ's presence that, sadly, in my experience, are rare qualities.

What you will find on the pages that follow are not the pontifications of a professional theologian but the honest reflections, insights and discoveries of a disciple of Jesus, excited by following him and learning more of him. My prayer is that as you read what Sal has written God will speak to you and as a result you will see a little more of Jesus and grow to be that bit more like him.

Steve Chalke
The Oasis Trust, London

Preface

The publishers asked me to write a book for young people about my life; I replied that I didn't think many people would want to read about the life of Sal Solo, but that I had gathered many more interesting stories during my life and travels. You have the result in your hands: fifteen thoughts, fifteen stories, fifteen prayers, and fifteen more prayers. I don't know why everything ended up in fifteens – there are even fifteen illustrations! – but I suppose if you read one a day, this book would last you three months – so long as you took weekends off! You may not find all of the pages to your liking, but I hope some of them will speak to you, as they have to those I have tried them out on.

My only reservation about having a book published is that some people may take that to mean my life is more important than theirs. Not so. Every life is equally important to God, who created it – my life has simply been *different* . . .

Sal Solo
London, 1992

Fifteen Stories

of things that
have happened to me

A Piece of Scribble

I was recording in France, and the record producer had a small four-year-old son who would hang around the studio quite often. I speak French to a reasonable level of conversation, but bearing in mind that we might often have trouble understanding a small child speaking our own language, I was pretty unsure about communicating with a four-year-old in a foreign tongue!

I know that kids usually like being picked up, and if you play simple games with them, you can become friends, but what kind of things do you say to a little French boy? I sat him on my lap, and lifted him up, and played a few simple games, asking basic questions to see if he would understand me, like 'Qu'est que c'est?' (What's this?). To my surprise, I would get a response that I could understand, as he told me his slippers were rabbits, and so on!

By the second or third day we had become good friends, and I saw him passing something to his father, saying 'Un cadeau' (a

present). He then turned to me saying 'Un cadeau' as he passed me a small scrap of paper with scribble on it. It was only scribble that made no sense at all, but I was really pleased because that scrap of paper meant we had formed a relationship.

It later occurred to me that to God who made the world, and made us, all of our efforts to offer something to him must seem rather like that piece of scribble from a four-year-old. But God must react just the same way as I did to my 'cadeau' – it doesn't matter that it's only a piece of scribble, the fact we offer it means we have formed a relationship.

Trust

A close friend of mine, at the time we first met, said, 'You can't trust anybody.' He was in his mid-teens at the time, so I realised that he may not have formed any meaningful friendships yet, and perhaps had been let down so far. I, on the other hand, was much older, and had had good friendships through most of my life, so I knew that if we were to have a relationship, I would have to teach him to trust. The only way I know to teach anyone trust is by trusting them. Little by little I began trusting him with my feelings, experiences, and small personal things. Some years later I reminded him of our earlier conversation, by which time it was obvious we had both learned to trust each other.

That same friend had further problems on his own thorny path to maturity, in particular with his image among friends his own age – his peer group. He told me they all thought of him as hard, as perhaps a leader. I knew him to be quite a different person, sensitive, caring, and thoughtful – qualities that could be described as 'soft'. This affected his relationship with his girlfriend, because she obviously loved the soft, caring person he was to her, but then couldn't understand why he had to act the 'hard man' when his friends were around.

In a long conversation with his father once, I noticed something very interesting; his father would never use the word 'love'. No matter where the discussion led, he would not admit to loving anyone, or that anyone loved him, thinking the word too soft – he would only allow himself to use the word 'like'. I realised the man must have been hurt deeply somewhere along the way; perhaps he had been let down, or didn't really dare believe he was actually lovable. He had passed his own problem on to his son, brought him up to be tough because the world is a hard place.

One time this friend told me I was too soft with people, and allowed them to walk all over me. I replied that people didn't come to me for harsh treatment, they came for someone who would have time for them, to listen, to understand, perhaps to sympathise. In other words, they came to me because I am soft, and so perhaps that is my best attribute. Jesus was soft to the point of allowing himself to be punished for each of his friends. My friend has begun to realise it may take more courage to be soft than hard, because now he has learned to trust.

Spider

At a time when I was doing a lot of radio programmes, I was asked to do a Lent series for a local radio station. The idea was that each afternoon during Lent they would broadcast five minutes of me interviewing someone from the local community – from school, hospital, police, prison, or dockyard. It was quite an education as I only spent three days in the area, and didn't have time to be briefed on any of the individuals before the tape started rolling, and I had to get something interesting from them.

When it was time to visit the prison, I was a bit apprehensive. I had only once before been in a prison, and I was told at least one prisoner I would interview had killed someone – I didn't know which one. I was offered a cup of tea by one prisoner who looked a bit shifty-eyed, and was covered in tattoos. When it was his turn to be interviewed, he spoke in a soft, almost broken voice, and the story he told is one I will never forget.

As a child he was locked in a room for a year and a half, until a neighbour alerted a doctor. His parents were constantly fighting

5

before they split up; his father was drunken and violent, as was his mother's boyfriend later on, and the boy grew up as a violent youth, going from borstals to detention centres, and eventually to prison. At the time of the interview he was serving time for robbery. Not only was the story staggering, but his fragile voice seemed to be reliving the experiences.

Eventually, to try and make the interview less heavy, I asked if he had discovered anything he enjoyed doing in prison, and to my surprise he replied, 'Yes, I've become a Christian'. Well, that was an answer I could not have expected, and I went on to ask, now he believed in God, why he thought that God had allowed him to have such a terrible life. 'So I can use my experiences to help other people', he replied simply.

Some months later Spider came to visit me on his home leave, and after he had listened to our interview, I found him in tears. It was clear that he had really changed, and it taught me that even the worst things that happen to us in life can be turned around into something good.

The Punk Who Would Be a Priest

A friend of mine at the age of sixteen used to be a punk, dressed in leather and earrings, with makeup on his face, and a mohican hairdo. He was constantly getting drunk and fighting. One weekend he decided to go with some mates to a retreat in a monastery – they thought it might be 'good for a bundle'. When they arrived though, they couldn't quite get over how genuinely kind people seemed to be there.

One time my friend punched someone in the face, and got the response: 'Jesus loves you'. He was really taken aback, and somehow ended up alone in the chapel, trying to make sense of all of this. He didn't know why he was there, and didn't understand what was happening to him. Whether he actually knew how to make a prayer or not, I don't know, but he felt he couldn't move, and believed he saw Jesus beckoning to him.

When he was eventually able to get up, it seemed as though

all the violence and aggression inside him had gone. He knew he could never be the same again, and felt directly called to follow Christ in an active way, and become a minister. He was a member of the Church of England, but his initial attempts to get into the priesthood met with great difficulty: he was young, a punk, and had no special academic qualifications.

It is easy to see why the Church authorities may have viewed such a candidate with suspicion: maybe it was just a passing fad, and in a year or two he would forget all about God. However, he persisted, and after long years of study, he was ordained as an Anglican priest. He still wears earrings and leather, but the mohican is gone now!

This is a true story . . . it may not be as a priest or minister, but in your ordinary day to day life, could Christ be calling you in some way to follow him?

Affirmation

My father was rather eccentric, and believed that money was for saving up, but never for spending, and as a result, the houses I grew up in didn't have many basic home comforts. The walls inside and out were undecorated, there were few carpets in the house, no central heating, and an outside toilet. My father used to criticise those who lived in council houses, but I dreamed of carpets, tiled bathrooms and an inside toilet like they had! I didn't like my schoolfriends to know where I lived because one time, after a friend I valued had turned up unexpectedly on the door-step, other people at school began to say my family must be gypsies because we lived in a shack.

Recently a friend told me that he lacked confidence because his schoolfriends always put him down, and excluded him from everything. He came from a very privileged background, and even though it was a private school he went to, he didn't like people to see his home, in case the sight of such a big house, and such affluence, gave them further ammunition to throw at him.

7

Isn't it strange that no matter what your situation or background, others seem to be able to find something to use against you, particularly when you're at school? It's almost as though everyone must make up for their own insecurities by making others feel bad, but as no one is exempt, we're creating a never-ending circle of hang-ups throughout the world.

Americans often use a word which is more unfamiliar to the English – it's 'affirmation'. It means literally 'to agree' but in practice, affirmation means someone telling you that 'You're all right', that 'I accept you', that 'I'm pleased to call you my friend'. Jesus constantly affirmed people and told them they were all right with him. If we are to be like Christ, perhaps we need to counter-act that negative circle of insecurity with a circle of affirmation.

8

The Boy on the Train

I was on a train in Scotland, and a boy got on and sat opposite. I saw him out of the corner of my eye, but didn't look up as I was reading. I soon began to think how reserved are we British, that we would sit for an hour with someone and never even say a word. I thought he could even be a Christian, and I may well have said a little silent prayer that we might make contact. Very soon, the boy said, 'Excuse me, are you a Christian?' He had spotted my pocket Bible. We spent the rest of the journey talking about our faith, before being abruptly interrupted by my stop, and I got off without even knowing his name.

Some time later, I had lost my address book, and I had it returned by a priest I know in Birmingham. There was a covering letter from a Scottish student saying he had found it on a train after talking to someone about the Christian faith. There was no identification on the book, so he had sent it to the first priest's address he found inside. He said the man he talked to had no hair, and wore a cap . . . 'Perhaps you know him?' The description left no doubt, and I was able to write and thank the boy, having now discovered his name and address.

One day I came home to find a couple of boys with rucksacks waiting on my doorstep, one of whom told me he was the boy from the train. He had been on a mission in Europe, and I invited him in for a meal. Since then we have kept in touch over a number of years, and it has often occurred to me that the only reason we ever met was because of our shared faith in Jesus Christ.

The Dead Body

I have not seen many dead bodies in my time. My mother died suddenly when I hadn't seen her for about six weeks, and the following day I was asked to identify the body as a formality. I went into a large, cold room in her local hospital, and there were a couple of policemen standing nearby. In the centre of the room was the body with a large cloth covering all except the head. I was rather surprised because it didn't look like my mother. Apart from how white the face was, and the fact that she usually wore glasses and the corpse had none, somehow the bone structure and even the shape of her nose looked different. It was all more angular and bony.

I said to the policemen, 'I suppose it must be her, but it doesn't look like her.' In fact, the only thing that made the likeness certain was her hair – she used to dye it a reddish shade, and it was a bit thin and wispy – that hadn't changed. The policemen said if there was even the slightest doubt, then they should get someone else to identify the body, so my sister-in-law did. Of course there was no doubt who it was, the body was found in my mother's bathroom, and she had died of natural causes, but I couldn't get over how different the dead body looked from my mother when she was alive.

I was later telling this story to my sister and by that time had realised the reason. Our bodies are only shells, and what we see in the glimmer of our eyes, in a smile or in the personality of each individual is really just a glimpse of the soul – that most important immortal part that God has given us. I didn't recognise my mother in that dead body because she was no longer there – the real person of my mother had been liberated from that frail, ageing body to join her maker!

It made real sense of the words I have often heard read at funerals: 'Life has changed, not ended.' In a sense, her life had just begun – eternal life with Christ!

The Red Spot

I used to have a musician in my band who was Indian, and a Hindu. I was offered a meal at his house one day, but then discovered I was the only one eating; he and his wife said it was

10

a fast day. Well, I sometimes fasted too, and so we began talking about our different faiths. They then opened a cupboard in the wall which contained an altar, including a picture of Jesus. They said they prayed to Jesus on a Wednesday because when they were in Bombay, everyone went to a big service at a Christian Church on a Wednesday. Well, it's a start I thought, and perhaps there will come a time when they will be able to pray to Jesus any day of the week!

Much later we were playing at a large Christian festival, and before going on stage, my Indian musician put a red spot on his forehead. This created much interest among the other members of the band, and he explained it was blessed wax from his temple, and he put it on so that God would be with him in the performance. I thought that was rather nice – I had a cross in my pocket as a sign that God would be with me too.

As it was the first time I had ever played to a specifically Christian audience, I thought perhaps they should hear this story, to know that even a Hindu had asked God to bless this performance, and so perhaps we could find some common ground with others of God's people. Shortly afterwards my performance was cut short, and a BBC producer later told me that people backstage were panicking in case I said anything more controversial.

This all happened some years ago now, and even though I believe more firmly than ever that it is through Christ we are saved, I am also more aware than ever of his command to love our neighbour as ourselves. We do not love others by condemning them, and we do not convert others by threatening them. We must meet them where they are at, as Christ did, and if we begin with what we have in common, then I suspect it will be much easier to sort out the things which divide us.

Who Are the Poor?

Without realising it, my journey towards God began long before the day in a hotel room when I asked him to make himself known to me. When I travelled the world in search of adulation, I saw

the effects of war and greed. I saw tanks in Yugoslavia long before their civil war began; I saw people queueing for bread in communist countries, and child prostitutes in Thailand. In Mexico I noticed that the poor live in corrugated huts with no windows, but with a TV aeriel on top, as they can receive American TV channels.

The deepest impression of all was from India. The house I grew up in was poor by western standards, but I had never before slept in a hotel room when outside hundreds of others were sleeping on·the street pavement, or, if they were lucky, on a wheelbarrow that someone had left. You cannot travel anywhere in the streets of India without being approached by beggars, often children, but even if you give them something they don't go away – rather you will find ten more tugging at your clothes in a few minutes.

Neither I nor any of the members of my band were Christians at the time, but on the way home we couldn't help talking about how we in the West use the word 'poverty'. In Britain poverty might be having a black and white TV or no car. Even in these days of recession, the unemployed can receive state benefits. The people we had seen in India had absolutely nothing, not even clothes, and no prospect of ever having anything. I was surprised when I talked about it to Indians in this country that many of them did not seem to care; they accepted it as being normal.

Over the past few years I have been involved in one way or another with a project called Christmas Cracker which mobilises young people to raise money for the poor, especially children in the Third World. I can never stress enough the importance of such initiatives. Some people will say we should look after our own poor first as an excuse for doing nothing. But the Third World population *are* our poor and they have become poorer while we have become rich and fat at their expense. We have plundered their resources without paying them the price, and Jesus told us we would be called to account for it in the end. The poverty we know in this country is different altogether, and needs to be addressed too, but please spare a thought for our Third World brothers and sisters.

13

Lessons in Love

Someone I know contacted me wanting to call round for a rare visit – I might usually only see him once every year or two. We had never discussed his sexuality, although I knew many people took him to be gay from his appearance. He told me he had split up with a bloke he had lived with for two or three years, and he was going through a hard time as a result. He talked romantically about their time together as having been absolutely perfect.

I felt he perhaps needed bringing back down to earth, and suggested first of all that if it had been so perfect, then it would not have ended after two or three years of 'honeymoon period' – that suggests romance or infatuation, not love. Love is not always about having a good time, or being on an eternal high; love may involve hardship and suffering and still survive despite the problems that come along. I happened to know his parents were happily married, and gave them as an example of what love is really all about. 'They must have had hard times bringing you and the rest of your family up', I suggested. 'It can't have been all plain sailing over the years, but they're still together, and that's what love is really all about.'

For once I had hit the right chord with him, as, to my surprise, he went on to say that his parents had actually split up for some years when he was young, but they had eventually got back together – they couldn't stay apart – and now, they were still very much in love. He could see they had indeed gone through hardship, and their life together certainly had not always been a bed of roses, but they had gone far beyond romance to real deep love.

I'm not sure I succeeded in convincing him that in my view he was unlikely to ever find the kind of real love we were talking about in a homosexual relationship, but at least for a few moments he could see the difference between love and romance. If only he could have seen also that God loved him still through all his

14

pains and loneliness, perhaps he could also have discovered that higher love that makes sense of all our other relationships.

My Boots

One time when I was visiting a place for youth retreats, I sat in on a service with a friend. There were three groups of sixth-formers taking part, from Plymouth, Liverpool, and I think somewhere around Gloucester. The sixth-formers had already been there at least a day before us, and so many had already got to know one another a little. We were introduced by our first names, with no more said about us, and so we sat quietly taking in what was going on. I assumed my name would have meant nothing to the young people, as I hadn't made a record or been on TV for a few years at that time.

After the evening's proceedings had come to an end, one boy made a beeline for me, and I wondered what he was about to say. 'Excuse me, mate, where did you get those great boots from?' Well, the boots were nothing special – I'd bought them in a sale in Oxford Street, and I'd certainly made no special effort to dress up that evening. It told me a great deal about communication though, because my personal choice of what was comfortable and suited me was the same as that eighteen year old's.

I was telling this story later to somebody who had been a Methodist youth worker, and he said the problem is often that youth workers are trained in how to communicate with the young, and they try to adopt trendy clothes, or catchphrases, but end up failing miserably because it's false. You don't have to *be* a young person to reach the young, you just have to be yourself and they will respect your honesty. It's much better that you offer them something of your experience as an adult, and at the same time let them know you accept them as they are, without having to conform to older people's expectations.

Having thought about this story, I realise that like an eternal teenager, I still enjoy funny clothes and fashion; I'm just as interested in music and what's in the charts as I ever was as a

15

teenager, and I hope I have held on to that idealism that is so often beaten down by disappointments, or turns to cynicism as we get older. But now I have the benefit of many years more experience too, and that's what I'd like to be able to pass on to the young.

Call You By Your Name

I must have signed thousands of autographs during my career. At its peak, there were often so many people pushing for a signature that only the few at the front could obtain it. I never quite understood the significance of my autograph to the people taking it away. Was it so they could prove they had met a singer? Was it just a reminder of an enjoyable event, like a snapshot might be? People who have known me in ordinary life have often been surprised that others might come up and ask me to sign a bit of paper – to them, I'm just the same as everybody else!

I once watched a TV discussion about the obsession of fans with their heroes, who may be singers, actors, or TV personalities. The Clint Eastwood movie *Play Misty for Me* illustrates it well, and I have myself been subjected to obsessive approaches and frequent marriage proposals from ladies I don't know at all. In the TV discussion, a psychologist said there are people who have difficulty with real-life relationships, and so prefer a lover who cannot answer back, who they can switch on and off with the turn of a button. They sometimes even send demands and meeting arrangements to the stars who cannot answer back, and then become angry when the stars don't respond.

Really though, everyone is more happy to have a relationship with someone they know, and who knows them – otherwise it's not really a relationship at all. I was discussing with a young Polish priest the changes of attitude towards the Church among the young in Poland since the downfall of Communism. I asked him what kind of Church young people in Poland now wanted. The

priest replied, 'They want a Church which, like Jesus, calls them by their own name.'

Isn't that what we all really want, not a one-sided fantasy relationship, not someone who cannot answer back, but someone who knows our own difficulties, hurts, and problems, and answers them?

Twins

A friend of mine had twins. One baby died after thirty hours and the other is still alive and healthy. She carried both of them for nearly nine months, and so her joy at the birth was as great as her grief over the death of one baby. It is difficult to say whether or not it might have been easier for her if the baby had died at birth, before she had the chance to hold it, feed it, and change it for a whole day and a half. Or did the chance to have just a little time with that baby provide a little comfort? I could offer no profound words when she grieved over the baby she lost, as I cannot imagine what it must be like for a woman to carry two babies around inside for nearly nine months, and then see one die.

She asked me to arrange for a priest friend to conduct the funeral, and he told me he found it so difficult to know what to say: 'How do you explain to people why God allows such things to happen?' I did not attend the funeral, but sent a card on which I wrote a simple inscription that made my answer clear: 'One baby got eternal life – the other has a life on earth first. I'm not sure which one got the best deal.'

Really, I am sure which one got the best deal – the one who received eternal life immediately. If you ask any child would they like a present today or next week, they will almost certainly answer 'today'. So why then if we really believe God's promises to us, should we consider God cruel when he gives us our reward sooner rather than later? Could it be that we simply don't really have enough faith to believe him?

Games

In the street where I grew up, there were no other kids. My father was very old and didn't take part in any physical activities – he only liked to watch boxing on the TV. I had no older brothers near my age, and no uncles or male family friends, so consequently I never learned to kick a ball around or any of those other games that boys usually enjoy.

I remember at the age of about seven, our first football lesson came about at school. When the teacher announced we were going to play football, he got an excited cry of approval from the boys, as they ran off kicking the ball. I was left puzzled as to what was happening, and to this day I've never learned all the rules of the game. What a pity that teacher was insensitive to the tiny minority who needed coaxing, instead of only noticing the majority who didn't really need teaching what they had already learned.

The result was that I went through my school days believing there was no point in making any effort in sports because I was bound to fail, when all the other kids were naturals. Many people have a similar attitude towards the Christian lifestyle – they believe there's no point in trying, because they're bound to fail.

I only finally got to kick a ball around in later life when my friend's small sons insisted I play football with them, and as they were young and no doubt as ignorant of the rules as me, there seemed no risk of failure or rejection in playing. I quite enjoyed myself because for the first time I realised it doesn't matter too much if you're any good or not – taking part is enough.

Jesus said we must become like little children to enter the Kingdom of Heaven. Perhaps he meant that, like kids, we need not be afraid of failing, our willingness to try will be enough, and we may even learn all we need to know just by taking part.

Christians Don't Like Animals

I used to know a girl who had two dogs, four cats, and also supported the upkeep of some animals in London Zoo. She didn't believe in God, and one day told me that Christians don't like animals, because we say they have no souls. Clearly the girl found some comfort in relating to animals that perhaps she didn't find with people, and certainly didn't find in God. I have often thought back to her comment since then, when I have seen people showing disrespect to any of God's creatures, and also when hearing of animal rights campaigners poisoning chocolate bars and so on – they seem to have something rather out of perspective.

It is true we don't believe animals have souls – nothing in the Bible suggests they do, but Jesus told us his Heavenly Father looks after them, and he often used animals to illustrate points about human beings. Of one thing I'm certain, that if we believe God created everything, including nature, and animals, we should have even greater respect for them than non-believers, so though we may be accused of many things, I don't think all Christians can be said to dislike animals.

Having said all that, I've personally never been too keen on dogs and cats: partly because dogs often jump all over me, and cats tend to want to sit on my lap and dig their claws in. Someone told me that they only do that when they know you don't like them. So cats dig their claws in me because I don't like them, and I don't like them because they dig their claws in! That certainly has a moral for our relationship with God and with other people. Many people think God doesn't love them, or is not interested in them, and so don't love or take an interest in him. They are wrong, he loves you, and is interested in everything about you, no matter how small.

As for our relationship with others: we all send out a vibe to the people we meet, it may say 'Welcome', it may say 'I'm embarrassed', it may even say 'I'm not interested in you'. When the other person picks up on that vibe, it's very difficult for them not to send the same vibe back. Well, someone has to break this circle, so it's my new resolution to try and send off an 'I'm interested in you' vibe to whoever I meet now, and just see what happens . . .

Fifteen Thoughts

Short Ideas with
Messages

Ideas of God

God is the one who always knows the answer when I don't.

God is the one who gives us teeth and gives us bread.

God is the one who stands at the door, knocks and waits, however long it takes for us to answer.

God is the friend I have always looked for, who is always there when I'm most in need, and understands how I feel. I don't have to feel embarrassed to explain, as he already knows.

God is also there when I'm most happy, but I may forget he's responsible.

God is the one who started it all off, and keeps it all going.

God is seen by some as an old man with a grey beard, but to me he just looks good!

God is the one who, when we ask for something, usually gives us something better, but we don't always recognise it at the time.

God is the one who some call Allah, others Jehovah, but he calls us all by our own name.

God is the only worthwhile reason to have, hold, love and cherish.

God is the father of our Lord Jesus Christ.

God is the centre of my life.

Hugs

Contrary to popular belief, boys like to be hugged! Some years ago I was staying at a home in New York for teenage boys who may have had drugs, drink, or domestic problems. One boy told me he had been on a 'Hugs' weekend – 'It was great!' He said he had stood in a circle, and everyone had to say something good about him, then they all hugged. 'It was great', he said again, and this was a boy some may have found tough or antisocial!

When I started going to Evangelical churches, I noticed how many people hugged each other upon meeting, and thought it a bit 'over the top'. That is, until they began hugging me, and I felt welcomed and accepted. Sometimes actions say more than words, and it's no good saying, 'I'm happy to see you', while extending an outstretched arm and keeping them at a distance; when you embrace them, they will really believe you're pleased to see them!

I've sometimes tried it out on people I'm not particularly fond of, or pleased to see, not because I needed or wanted to, but because I felt they needed it. For instance, a boy who has had problems with a father figure not showing enough warmth may be reassured by an embrace from another man. This is common in continental cultures, but we Brits tend to be too reserved. At times of reconciliation, after an argument or shouting match with someone, rather than spending ages discussing the ins and outs, a simple hug may be much more eloquent.

There is also another reason this gesture may be well appreciated – in the case of single and unattached Christians, they may never have physical contact with others, and a hug is something non-sexual that lets them know they're not alone in life. We're all really babies wanting to get back to the womb, so perhaps that's why boys like hugs!

A Precious Pearl

Each one of us has inside what I call our 'precious pearl' – a small gem that consists of everything that's most personal and sensitive to us, sitting in our soft centre. Pearls are naturally to be found resting in the soft centres of oysters and I believe we also have a strong desire to find a resting place for our precious pearl within other people – to share our burdens and our secrets.

But not all shells belong to oysters, even though they may look similar on the outside, and the quest for a resting place for your precious pearl may result in rejection and hurt. How many times have you trusted someone with your secrets only to find they didn't value what you were sharing with them? Only the right person will recognise the value of your precious pearl when it may not shine to the rest of the world.

This same problem applies to all our relationships, our loves and friendships. In order to achieve success, we must risk failure. I have often felt betrayed or let down having shared my love, my friendship, or my secrets with others. On the other hand though, many times that sharing has resulted in close bonds with others that are not easily broken, so I will go on risking my 'precious pearl' in other unknown resting places.

Jesus spoke about turning the other cheek, and about forgiving seven times seventy. I suspect it's because if we merely retreated every time we were hurt or disappointed, we could never build meaningful relationships with others, but if we can take the knocks and still try again, we may well turn others around.

God's Puppy

I think most people would say I'm fairly even-tempered, and not renowned for fits of rage or irrational reactions to difficult situations. I do on the other hand have a habit of making friends with people who have short tempers and are often flying off the handle! Perhaps it's true what they say about opposite poles attracting each other, and it could even be that we need each other for balance.

One particular friend of mine is a good Christian who reads the Bible, and tries very hard to improve his life as a result. The only thing is that he can't quite control his emotions, and he's inclined to get really upset in an instant over things someone else might just ignore, or shrug off. I've tried to tell him to look on these little trials as a gift from God – a chance to share a bit of Christ's sufferings, or even one of the thorns from his Crown of Thorns. All these small things can help build up our tolerance and charity towards others, and so in the end might do him the power of good.

He didn't seem to quite enthuse over these suggestions, so I came up with another idea. If you have a puppy it must be house trained, and that may involve rubbing its nose in its own mess in order to teach it the right habits. You are God's puppy, and so you have to be trained to live a perfect Christian life, sometimes through unpleasant experiences. At the end of the training though, you should find that living out the love, charity, tolerance and understanding required by a follower of Christ is not such an impossible effort after all.

My friend says he likes being God's puppy!

Batman

Lots of kids these days seem to look up to the likes of Kylie and Jason as their heroes, or maybe Madonna, Michael Jackson, or Prince. Some of the younger kids I've known over the years have been mad about everyone from Masters of the Universe, to Ninja Turtles, to Bart Simpson! Cast your mind back to when you were twelve years old . . . who was your hero, what was your favourite TV programme . . . what were your likes and dislikes? You should enjoy remembering those things, as everyone's favourite subject is themselves!

When I was twelve, my hero was Batman. I'm not quite sure why I much preferred him to Superman, Spiderman, or any of the other super-heroes of the day. I suppose there was an air of mystery about him, he always did good, always won, and he had funny gadgets to fit all situations. I remember his 'Utility Belt' that had a compartment to cope with every predicament.

Now I'm grown, my hero is Jesus, but he's not at all like Batman. God chose to save the world through suffering and apparent defeat. The Jesus who hung on the cross and died for us was no super-hero, no Batman – he was naked and shamed in front of everyone. In other ways though, the resurrected Christ is quite like Batman: he seems to have a solution, always for the better, and he will always win in the end.

I suppose I'd have to say that's why now Jesus is my Batman.

The Family of Christ

There was a family: mother, father and four children. The parents had their disagreements from time to time, but usually managed to sort things out, sometimes reaching agreement with the whole family. A time came though, when the arguments seemed more common, and a general attitude of antagonism became the norm. She felt he did not take her seriously because she was a woman, and he resented her apparent desire to manipulate the children.

One day tempers flared up into such a disagreement that mother and father stopped talking to one another. Neither one had anywhere else to go, so they carried on living in the same house together, but never again spoke to each other. The oldest daughter was closest to her father, but the other three children were closer to the mother, so when the kids returned from school that day, three of them sided with their mother, leaving the oldest girl isolated in support of her father. So the family was really split in two: father and daughter keeping to themselves, mother and three other children not speaking to the others.

In due course the oldest son began to have regular arguments with his mother: the older he became, the more old-fashioned and simple she seemed. One day he declared he would not accept her authority any more, and though still living in the same house, he would have nothing more to do with her. When the two younger kids returned from school, one sided with the mother, and the other with the brother, so now there were three separate divisions in the household, each one angry with the others, and each one feeling justified in their anger.

Eventually the children got married, and according to which side of the family feud they were on, their children were brought up believing the others to be completely wicked, and their own parents completely justified. Some of them even built houses facing one another, and yet never spoke a word to them. As the years passed, the original arguments became blurred or forgotten, but everyone believed there must have been very good reasons,

31

and that the others could never change anyway. Occasionally one of the grandchildren might wonder, 'Is my grandmother really such a witch? Could my grandad be as bad as they all say?' But they were never to find out because the divisions were drawn, and no one ever crossed over.

Now do you suppose this is a family that pleased God? Could this ever be offered as an example of how a Christian family should live? It is however the way *the* Christian family has lived. The father in this story is called Orthodox, and the mother, Rome. The oldest son is Reformer, and the grandchildren are us, the members of the various Churches. Are the others really as bad as they say? What were the reasons we all originally fell out, and do those reasons still exist? Isn't it time that we, the family of Christ, started to put our own house in order?

Respectable People

There was once a man, son of an unmarried mother, born in such poverty, they didn't have beds to sleep on. His family had to escape from the authorities to another country, and even when they returned, they couldn't go home, in case they were caught.

He had no special education, but, at the age of twelve, he was able to give his teachers a good run for their money in an argument. He was taught to be a craftsman by his foster father, but when he had grown up he suddenly gave up work and started to roam around the country.

In no time, he was encouraging others to do the same, and spending all his time with crooks and winos, prostitutes and people with AIDS. Most respectable people didn't want anything to do with him: 'He's telling everyone to give away their money, when we've spent years building up fortunes! He's telling them everyone's equal; what will happen to our positions? We must put a stop to it!'

They executed him with no proper trial while he was still young, but instead of that being the end, people began talking about strange powers released after his death. The respectable people didn't see them though; they were too busy with their businesses and their fortunes.

They still don't take any notice today, and even if some of them go once a week to pay homage to the man they killed, they make sure it won't affect their lives in any way.

If that same man walked down our main streets today, who would follow him? Would it be winos and crooks? Would it be priests and ministers? Would it be the respectable people? Would it be you and I?

Which One Was Me?

On my first album in 1981, I was pictured in heavy make-up and a cloak, against an exotic tropical background. For my second album a year later, the cloak had been replaced by black leather, and the exotic background had become folds of white silk – something like an expensive brothel I suppose, although I've never been in one! By the next album I had switched to suits, and began covering my shaven head with a hat. The image was always changing, but which one was me?

In concert I never spoke a word to the audience, preferring to keep a remote and mysterious image, but in interviews, people were surprised how chatty I was, and how different to the stage image. Which one was me? On foreign tours, our audiences often numbered 10,000 and I remember on one occasion we had an audience of 25,000 in a park in Helsinki – from the stage we could only see heads in every direction. Thousands bought my records and even put my posters on their walls – in cloaks, in leather, in suits, but which one was me? The answer is none of them, as it was all an illusion; just an attempt to create a larger than life character to hide the fact I was really just the same as everyone else who bleeds, hurts, and needs.

What of all those audiences today – where are they now? I doubt that many of you reading this can even remember any of the things I describe above. That's because I was selling a lie. The larger than life character had no power to change people's lives,

and for all the money people spent on my records and concerts, they got back little of value. In effect I let them down, and so they moved on to other idols.

It is only in worshipping Christ that all your needs will be answered. He is the only one who will not let you down, and will never fail to deliver the goods. Don't waste your time and money chasing idols when only God can meet your needs – and he offers you salvation for free!

A Special Cocktail

Some people seem to think the fifties or sixties might have been more exciting times to live in – more original fashions, better music perhaps. Do you ever wish you had been born in another time? Maybe you sometimes dream of living in a more exotic country, and when you have arguments at home, you might well begin to wish you were born into a different family.

Well, at the beginning of time, I believe God must have been able to see everyone who would ever exist, and he began to spin that intricate web of circumstances that would make each life in some way affect, and in other ways, rely on, other people. He could then have caused you to be born at any time in history; in another part of the globe; to different parents, and with totally different talents and abilities . . . but then you wouldn't be you, would you?

Even if you had a twin, the two of you would be separate individuals, no matter how close you may feel, because you are *unique* – you are one of a kind, and there never has been, and never will be, another like you. Your own life's experiences, your particular talents and personality; your own friends, your own hopes and aspirations, and how you relate to all these things – that's what makes you *you*. I call it your 'special cocktail'.

Now if God gave you all this equipment, and also mapped out the events and opportunities that would happen only in your life, then perhaps he also planned certain things that only you can do. How could anyone else do them, when they don't have that

35

same special cocktail? So you see, if you miss those unique opportunities that were made only for you because you're too busy trying to be somebody else, it would be a tragedy, wouldn't it . . . those special moments in history that can never be repeated?

Personally I wouldn't have minded being Michael Jackson – not for his money or fame particularly, but because he has a good voice, dances well, and could almost be described as the perfect pop star. I don't look anything like Michael Jackson though, and couldn't even sing a note like him if I tried, still less dance like him. So if I had spent my career trying to be him, then I could at best only have even ended up as a poor second. As myself though, I'm the best because that's who I was made to be. As you, you're number one too, so don't be distracted from appreciating that special cocktail that God made only for you.

Many Rooms

Jesus said, 'There are many rooms in my Father's house.' Well, I think we all have many rooms inside. When we are young, we tend to live in maybe just one or two. In the same way as our bedroom may be our own special domain in the family home, and if left alone in the house, we might even be a bit frightened of venturing further afield or going where it's dark, we can be rather afraid of investigating the 'other rooms' inside ourselves.

The house I live in has three storeys and I rarely go upstairs, but of course I know exactly what's up there. Imagine though if I only explored one room at a time, how long it might take to get to know all the eleven or twelve rooms in the house.

At adolescence we suddenly discover the house inside ourselves is full of rooms, and, being frightened by the unknown, we retreat into the safe haven of the rooms we know. If we behave as our friends do, and agree with them, that's safe. If we act in a certain way all the time it's less frightening than exploring all those hidden emotions, fears and hangups; maybe even the softer sentimental parts – the 'rooms' that all go to make up our own unique house.

As we get older though, bit by bit we have to go into those rooms, and maybe even give them a spring clean – chuck out the rubbish, and make use of them. The only thing that's frightening about a dark room is that we may not know what lurks there. But once the light shows us everything that's hidden there's no longer any need to be afraid. Jesus can be the light we need to make all the rooms in our house bright and lived in. It's very difficult to manage a whole house, so we might do better to give the management of it over to him!

More Rooms

The statement 'There are many rooms in my Father's house' has another interpretation for me. A friend who had been away at college asked me, 'Did you miss me?' I tactfully avoided answering directly as I knew she would not like my answer. This evasion did not go unnoticed, and so, as she insisted, I answered in this way: 'I have many friends and I enjoy their company when I am with them. I can't be with all of them all of the time. So when I am with a particular friend I enjoy that, and when I'm with somebody else, I don't pine for the friend who is elsewhere. It's like during my professional career, people used to ask me whether I preferred concerts or recording and I would reply that I enjoy each one when I'm doing it, and don't think of the other.'

Another friend who had broken off an engagement told me he realised he would always have a 'room' in his heart for that girl which would not be filled by anyone else, and when he met the girl he would marry, she would simply occupy a different room in his heart.

I told him that I have a special room in my heart for him which cannot be occupied by anyone else, and indeed the same goes for each of my friends. The relationship we share with every friend is quite unique and unlike any other: the subtleties, the things we laugh at, the secrets, the understanding – none of these can be exactly duplicated with a different friend, no matter how close.

Jesus asked us to love each person as ourselves. Is your heart big enough to hold a room for everyone you meet? I think it is, and if you don't extend your love to others, then your house will simply be a collection of empty rooms with nobody's name on the door.

The Hours in a Week

How many hours in a week? Well 7×24 hours $= 168$. How do you spend your 168 hours? Let's suppose you sleep 8 hours a day, which will make 56 over a week. You might spend at least 14 hours eating, maybe more. We will assume you work a 40 hour week, or spend a similar amount of time at college, studying, revising, etc. You may have to travel a couple of hours each day, so that adds 14 hours to our total. Then there's TV; apparently the average Brit spends at least 20 hours a week watching the box – you might spend more!

All of those basics above add up to 144, leaving 24 hours free – like one day out of seven. Now, how much of that extra 24 hours do you give to God? Some people think they are generous to give one hour a week on a Sunday to go to church – many people can't even spare that. Perhaps you're one of those who's too busy? But even if you spent three hours every day on your favourite leisure activity, you would still have three hours left at the end for God . . . or would you?

Being too busy is a frame of mind. It's funny isn't it, how we always seem to find time for what's important to us, but things that take a little more effort, maybe we can't manage. Is God like one of those unpleasant chores we all put off to you? Well, maybe you need to get to know him better. If you took just 15 minutes a day to read the Bible, or even some other book about Christ, you might just find you want to know more about him. Some people have difficulty with reading, and might prefer to discover the good news by helping someone – visiting an old person, or whatever.

No matter what the perfect road to the Gospel for you, don't say you haven't the time . . . there are 168 hours in a week!

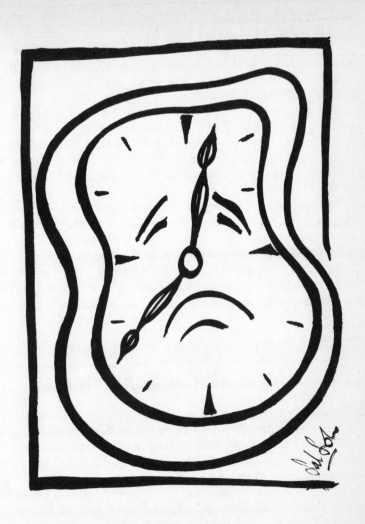

Sunday Best

If you were going out for the evening, whether to a restaurant, club or whatever, you might wear something special, perhaps put on a special perfume or aftershave, maybe wash your hair, or pay special attention to other features of your appearance. Many people would say it makes them feel better, but perhaps what they really mean is they think it will make them 'appear' better to others. If you were just staying at home to watch the TV with family or friends you would be unlikely to go to all that trouble because there would be nobody to impress.

In times gone by, people often went to a great deal of trouble dressing up to go to church on a Sunday – isn't that where the term 'Sunday best' came from after all? Today a few people still do, particularly in certain cultures, but for the most part, those in the west don't bother dressing up to impress a God they don't really believe exists.

Perhaps it's for the better, because our God cannot be easily deceived by what's on the surface. He cannot be bought or bribed either, and unlike humans, he cannot be flattered into ignoring our faults. The miracle is though, that he knows every one of our faults and failings better than we do ourselves, but he still loves us completely. If only we could learn to love ourselves as he loves us, just maybe we would no longer be satisfied with feeling better simply because we smell nice, or wear trendy clothes.

Jesus Christ Superstar

If I had been responsible for the plan to save the world, my saviour would probably have been a rock star. He would have had the most original music ever heard, the best songs, the strongest image, the greatest voice. His act would have been impossible for anyone else to imitate, and everyone would want to be like him. His followers would somehow have been able to take part in his glory, it would be reflected by them, and all the world would praise them for their wisdom and dedication in following him. He would have performed miracles and put all the wrongs of the world right; he would have had power beyond all others, and nobody could doubt his truth and greatness.

Perhaps your saviour would be similar to mine, but instead they would be a sports star, an actor, or whatever your interests would reflect. Our imagination is badly flawed though, and it simply shows how unlike God we are, and how human. God's plan of salvation goes against all human wisdom – he chose a suffering Christ who would be insulted and humiliated, whose followers would be laughed at for generations to come.

Following Christ goes against the grain of popular opinion, and it will seldom bring you success and fame in the eyes of the rest of the world. Christ added a couple of footnotes for believers though – he said we should store up our treasure in heaven, and that those who bear insults or persecution for his sake will have their reward. I still occasionally imagine my famous saviour for a few moments, but then I always come to the conclusion there would be little virtue in following the path everyone naturally chooses. That path leads to acclaim from other people, but to accept suffering or persecution gladly – now that really is something!

Gossip

Many people think the newspapers are getting worse and worse at prying into people's private lives and digging up the dirt. Their subject has to be someone famous though, as the public are not interested in hearing gossip about people they don't know unless the story itself is something quite extraordinary.

If you passed some people gossiping in the street and none of the names you heard were familiar, you would probably carry on without taking any further interest. If on the other hand you heard them mention someone you know, your ears might prick up, and you may even linger in the hope of hearing what they were talking about. I have often been the subject of gossip myself, because however untrue the stories may be, a false story about a name people may know will attract their interest much more than a true story about someone unknown.

In churches around the country, many people turn off the minute the priest, preacher or minister starts to talk about Jesus. Could it be that the talk is about someone they simply don't know? Perhaps every sermon should begin with the assumption the congregation may not personally know Christ, and even re-introduce him to them. Once the relationship is established, perhaps the people will be much more eager to hear about the sayings and doings of their new found friend!

Fifteen Prayers

For those who
would like to do more
than just read

Big Nose

There was once a man who had a very large nose. He felt so ugly that he used to take it out on other people. One day in the street, he passed a friend who had had a red rash come up all over his face. When this man stretched out his hand in friendship, the man with the nose shouted: 'Look how ugly you are with that red rash all over your face; I wouldn't be seen dead going out looking like that!' His friend went away in embarrassment, as all the passers-by looked on.

A week later, they met again in the street, but by this time, the rash had healed. Turning to the man with the big nose, the other said, 'Look how ugly you are with that big nose; my rash has

healed, but you'll always have that big nose!' Then the man with the big nose wished he had accepted the hand of friendship when it was first offered to him.

Many of us tend to judge people by the way they look, but God doesn't; looks change, but he always sees us as children, trying to find our way. We sometimes highlight other people's problems when we want to divert the spotlight away from our own; we can even delight in other people's troubles, and enjoy gossiping about them, as though it makes us feel better in ourselves, even if we call them our friends.

A true friend is someone who is quite aware of all your faults and failings, but loves you just the same, recognising that he or she has imperfections too. Jesus told the one without sin to cast the first stone when they had condemned the woman who had sinned, and he also said if we judge, we will be judged.

Jesus himself may not have had the faults you or I have, but he certainly knew rejection. When he carried his cross, Simon of Cyrene helped shoulder the burden, and Veronica wiped his face. Are we people who help others with their burdens, or who reject them and make them feel even worse, as though we were perfect ourselves?

'Do not judge, and you will not be judged; because the judgements you give are the judgements you will get, and the amount you measure out is the amount you will be given. Why do you observe the splinter in your brother's eye and never notice the plank in your own?' (Matthew 7:1–3)

Lord, help us not to judge others, so that you will not have to judge us.

Enough to Share

If you had a small packet of sweets in a room of people and it was a new packet, you would probably offer them around, knowing there would be some left afterwards. But if there were only two or three in the packet, you might fear there would be none left for yourself, and you would offer them to nobody. With things much more important than sweets, like love, joy, kindness, we sometimes do the same thing – instead of offering them around and sharing them with everybody, we may keep them to ourselves, or a select few, or maybe even only one other person – almost as though we feared there was not enough to go round.

The big difference though with love and its brothers and sisters is that when you offer it to others, it multiplies; in fact when shared, there's always more than enough to go round, but if you try to keep it to yourself, or perhaps share it with only one other person, then it's likely to wither and die. So be careful with your relationships – many young people expect their partner, boyfriend or girlfriend, to be everything to them. They may get possessive about their partners' friends, or make the mistake of spending all their time together, so that other friends end up being cut off. That's one sure way to stifle a relationship before its time!

When Jesus multiplied the loaves and fishes, I wonder if he intended a material illustration of what we are to do with our love. The disciples didn't think they would have enough for such a crowd, but they offered the little they had, and it never ran out. Let us offer the little we have too!

> Jesus said to them, 'How many loaves have you?' 'Seven', they said, 'and a few small fish.' Then he instructed the crowd to sit down on the ground, and he took the seven loaves and the fish, and he gave thanks and broke them and handed them to the disciples who gave them to the crowds. They all ate as much as they wanted, and they collected what was left of the scraps, seven baskets full. (Matthew 15:34–7)

Lord, help us to share the little love we have so it may be multiplied by you.

The Thing

The beautiful baby boy was growing into an inquisitive toddler. Everything that had caught his eye, but he couldn't previously reach, now became a goal. Nearly every inch of every room in the house seemed to be filled with wonder – a treasure trove of undiscovered delights! Spring brought interesting coloured things that smelled nice into the rooms, and summer brought strange flying visitors, some of whom made funny buzzing noises.

As autumn began to drift towards winter, a new delight grabbed his attention. It was different to everything else he had ever seen: a wonderful thing, bright and shiny, orange and gold. At first he could only gaze at it, transfixed, but then he wanted to reach out and touch it, he wanted to hold it and see what manner of thing it was, he wanted to possess such a thing of wonder! But the more he tried to get near it, the more his mother, or father, or anyone else in the house, seemed determined to stop him , no matter how hard he would scream or cry. It became a regular battle of wills, and whenever his attention would return to the wonderful thing, the more he would try, the more all the adults seemed determined to stop him getting near to it.

It was open day at the school, and although mum and dad didn't like leaving their little boy with a babysitter, they had to make sure his older brother and sister didn't feel neglected, and after all, a child has to get used to being without his family from time to time. The neighbour's daughter was a kind girl; a little scatty, but quite honest and trustworthy. Mum and dad told her to help herself to anything in the kitchen, and they'd be back by eight o'clock.

Half an hour passed without incident – only the girl and little boy in the house. 'Time for a cup of coffee', she said to him, 'and I'll get your milk.' Once she had left him playing with his toys, something caught his eye again: it was a wonderful thing, bright and shiny, orange and gold! Here at last was his chance, and he reached out towards the thing, to touch, to hold, to possess it. From the kitchen the girl heard an almighty scream and rushed back into the living room. The boy was impossible to console because the thing he had touched was called fire, and he had been burned.

But of the fruit of the tree in the middle of the garden God

48

said, 'You must not eat it, nor touch it, under pain of death.'
(Genesis 2:17)

Lord, help me to be able to take no for an answer.

The Root of the Problem

A friend of mine was living with her boyfriend. All was not well: he wanted to have children without being married, but she didn't want to bring more illegitimate babies into the world, not having had a father herself. As time went by, she realised her relationship was not right, and began to turn towards God. She came to the point where a decision had to be made about who was to be first in her life: she decided it was God, and set about planning to change her life. She began to pray regularly, and attend Christian events other than simply once on a Sunday.

The only problem was, she couldn't quite find the courage to deal with the most serious barrier to herself and God, and even though she hoped her boyfriend might himself follow her lead and become a believer, once something is freely given, it's rather difficult to take it away again. So she chipped away at the edges, trying to improve the little things in her life and their relationship, but the root problem remained unsolved. A couple of times she thought she had found the courage to break off the relationship and was determined to tell him, but he always semed to find a way of talking her round in the end. Although she said God was first in her life, in practice she placed the demands of her boyfriend first. The deadlines she set herself came and went, and the relationship continued.

Just chipping away at the outside without removing the root cause of sin can lead to serious problems though, as she discovered when she stopped taking the pill. She told her boyfriend she had stopped taking it, presumably in the hope it would make him respect her desire to live according to God's laws. This may seem to us too much to hope, but I'm sure she was sincere, if something of a dreamer. Within a couple of months she found herself pregnant, so her boyfriend had his original desire to have children without being married fulfilled, while she is even more separated from God, and the direction of her life is even more out of her control. The moral of this story is that you can't hope to keep one foot in the ways of the world, and the other in God's camp. If you want to follow God's son, Jesus Christ, don't hesitate or look back – it may sound difficult, but the rewards are plentiful!

> He said to them, 'I tell you solemnly, there is no one who has left house, wife, brothers, parents or children for the sake of the kingdom of God who will not be given repayment many times over in this present time and, in the world to come, eternal life.' (Luke 18:29–30)

Lord, give us the courage to place you first in our lives.

Do Babies Grow on Trees?

Some years ago, I remember listening to a fascinating talk by one of the world's top experts on pre-natal consciousness – that means the things we become aware of before we're born, from our mothers' wombs. He posed the apparently ridiculous question: 'Do babies grow on trees?' Well, the question proved not to be as ridiculous as it may have seemed on the surface.

Take the popular legend of babies being delivered by a stork – where does that come from? Well, apparently this idea came from an ancient native culture where they believed babies grew on trees, and were eaten by birds, who then delivered them as new babies.

In some Indian traditions, they planted a tree as a sign of fertility when they wanted a baby. Why do we have a Christmas tree to celebrate the birth of Christ as a baby in Bethlehem, and why was it in effect a tree on which Christ died, giving birth to the Church?

Well, the good doctor explained his theory that for nine months, in the warmth and security of our mother's womb, we receive all

our nourishment through a cord attached to what looks remarkably like a tree – a section of the placenta. After nine months, we're turfed out into the cold, the cord is cut, and in many of our habits, we spend the rest of our lives trying to get back into that warmth and security. Sounds a bit like Adam and Eve being thrown out of the garden of Eden, doesn't it?

To throw further light on the subject, the doctor said a baby can 'taste' the mood of the mother in the amniotic fluid – when she is content it tastes sweet, and when she's anxious or depressed, it is bitter. So an unwanted baby may even sense that it is not wanted before being born, while the child of a contented mother is likely to be quite happy. I immediately tested out this theory with a couple of my friends' babies – the mother of one really happy kid told me she had no problems during pregnancy, while another I knew to be born of an anxious mother was shy and nervous.

I have even heard of another doctor who has specialised in treating autistic children (those who do not communicate), by taking them back to the conditions of the womb, and creating a new loving environment. We all have times when we feel like trying to retreat to a more protected and comforting environment. I now realise though, that security can only be found in God. When he turned our first parents out of the garden of Eden, he had already formed the plan by which we would return to his presence – through his Son, Jesus Christ.

> So Yahweh God expelled him from the garden of Eden, to till the soil from which he had been taken. He banished the man, and in front of the garden of Eden he posted the cherubs, and the flame of a flashing sword, to guard the way to the tree of life. (Genesis 3:23–4)

Lord God, help me to find my security in you alone.

No Room

Very soon after I became publicly known as a Christian, I began to receive requests to visit schools, to talk about my faith. Since that time I don't know how many schools I have visited, but I usually combine music and video, and sometimes games and discussions with simple talking, and a great time is had by all. Although I occasionally speak to younger kids and even the odd primary school, fifth and sixth formers are my usual school audience.

After a while I started to question the effect of these visits: the teachers are usually very enthusiastic and assure me the kids will remember what I said for life – 'You'll never know the good you do'. But as the years have gone by, I have never been able to see even the slightest sign that this has led to a single person committing to Christ or even deepening their faith. Sometimes I have tried to follow up with prayer meetings and the response has been poor.

One time I remember a sixth former who even had his own car telling me he couldn't attend anything because of exams and studies. I was telling this story to Cardinal Hume, and he told me a similar one, of when he invited a sixth former to come and discuss something with him, but the student claimed to be too busy. 'I'm not asking you to stay a week', he had replied! We all know that few students spend every waking hour studying, and they can all make time for things they consider a priority, but obviously things connected to God don't usually fit into that category.

Most of the schools I visit are Catholic, and by piecing together my own experience as a pupil and later as an adult visitor, I have reached the following conclusion. Top priority in a Catholic school is usually given to passing the academic subjects which will lead to Higher Education, and ultimately a good job, and plenty of money. In other words, the clear message is *succeed in the world*. Matters of faith are often treated as optional, or as a duty, and so I reckon watching *Neighbours* or *Eastenders* is likely to rate higher than God in the minds of many young people.

Parents and teachers, what values are you passing on to the young? Young people, ask yourself how it is you can find time for many things in your life, except God? Remember, when he came into the world as a baby, no one had room for him.

'For if anyone is ashamed of me and of my words, of him the Son of Man will be ashamed when he comes in his own glory and in the glory of the Father and the holy angels.' (Luke 9:26)

Lord, help me to always find room for you in my life.

Sex

On the day I discovered God is not a myth, I also made another startling discovery: sex is not the most important thing in life (although in today's climate you might be forgiven for thinking it is!). Not that I had been especially promiscuous until then, but then most people spend more time thinking about it than doing it. Many people do it a lot because they're bored, depressed, or insecure and in need of love. Some people think they are unlovable, or at any rate don't believe they will ever find true love, so they settle for sex instead. Some people have sex with many people in search of love, but the more sex they have, the less they seem likely to ever find love.

That is why God is much more important than sex – he is the only one who can give us all the love we will ever need, and he is also the only one who can enable us to love the unlovable. What makes a Mother Teresa give her life to the dying in Calcutta? What made Francis of Assisi give everything he owned to the poor? Certainly not sex, but a divine love which sets us free of the simple cravings of our body. Not that sex is always evil – it is a gift from God when combined with true love, but divorced from love, it becomes the opposite. They say love and hate are very close, as it's easy to hate a lover who has jilted you, and the difference between 'love' and just 'making love' is just as drastic.

How many broken homes, how many divorces, how many abortions, and how many delinquent children have been the result of the absence of love? Yet there most certainly has been no absence of sex in those situations – begin to see what I mean? Personally I am single, as if God made a partner for me, I have not yet found her, so I will wait until I do rather than take second best. I would see little point in just having sex when what I really want is love. If God did not make a partner for me, then I'm happy to be single, as I know he has planned to give me all the love I need from elsewhere.

'For the one who asks always receives; the one who searches always finds; the one who knocks will always have the door opened to him. Is there a man among you who would hand his son a stone when he asked for bread? . . . If you, then, who are evil, know how to give your children what is good, how much more will your Father in heaven give good things to those who ask him!' (Matthew 7:8–11)

Lord, may I never settle for less than you.

Doctorin' The Tardis

Although I sometimes return to schools to address different classes, it's quite rare for me to see the same class more than once. There was an occasion though, when my visit to a sixth form raised many questions and they asked me back to answer them. They supplied them written in advance, which was the only time I've had that! Presumably, the idea was that I could avoid any I didn't like, or found embarrassing, but in the event, the two most potentially embarrassing questions were the ones I most wanted to answer.

The first read 'Did you give up music because your music was so bad?' and the second was 'If Bros asked you to join them, would you give up God?' I didn't think they had actually heard my music, so didn't take it as a personal appraisal of my art, but rather posed another question to them: 'Anyone know what's number one at the moment?' At that time it was a record called *Doctorin' the Tardis* which crossed Doctor Who with Gary Glitter! The class all laughed, and none of them thought that it was a brilliant record. I asked them what was the previous number one, and it was something they found even more embarrassing. So I didn't have to say a great deal more before they realised success is not necessarily any gauge of quality.

As for the question about Bros, they were riding high in the affections of teenage girls at that time, but I asked them if they could remember who occupied that slot a year before, or even the year before that. They had great difficulty remembering names like Curiosity Killed the Cat, King, and Kajagoogoo, even though each one had been just as popular as Bros a few years earlier. Bros have already been replaced as the heart-throbs of many by much newer acts.

I told the sixth formers that during my years in pop music, I had seen many bands and singers come and go, rise from nowhere, and fall just as quickly, but Jesus is for all time. He told us he is the Alpha and Omega, the beginning and the end. When all of the names above are long forgotten, he will still be there, and I would rather be number 10,000,000 in Heaven than number one in the Top 20!

> 'Do not store up treasures for yourselves on earth, where moths and woodworms destroy them and thieves can break in and steal. But store up treasures for yourselves in heaven, where neither moths nor woodworms destroy them and thieves cannot break in and steal. For where your treasure is, there will your heart be also.' (Matthew 6:19–21)

Lord, help me to set my sights on your Top 20.

Do Me a Favour

When I was a teenager, although I was a bit of a rebel in my appearance and attitudes, I went to church every week, and was probably considered a good Christian by older churchgoers as a result. I really knew nothing about the Christian faith at that time though, and I was certainly unaware that it was possible to really know God for yourself.

I think like many other young people, I associated everything dull and boring with God, and I imagined anything I enjoyed must be at least slightly wicked! Having been brought up from an early age to say prayers before going to bed, not believing they ever benefited me personally; and being told about sin offending God, and our 'duty' to go to church, I must have really thought God was some old misery who had to be constantly pacified.

Well, I would now like to share with you a startling discovery
I made a few years ago which is so important that I often repeat
it two or three times when I visit schools and youth groups:
When we pray, we don't do God any favours! Shall I repeat
that? When we pray, we don't do God any favours! If God does
actually exist, then he made the world, and us, so what favour
can you or I possibly do for him? The thought that God is in
some way satisfied by endless repetition of meaningless words is
ludicrous isn't it?

Who are the ones who really need the favours? Surely that's

us! So you see, the real purpose of praying is to give God the chance to do us a favour, because if we take time to talk and listen to him, we can tell him our problems and needs, and he may well give us the answers; but if we make our prayers begrudging sets of words repeated endlessly, then what good can that possibly be to anybody?

We should also remember to thank God for the things we have received, if only for our own benefit, to remind ourselves of all our blessings, and who is responsible for them. Next time you pray, remember, it's for your benefit, not God's!

'In your prayers do not babble as the pagans do, for they think that by using many words they will make themselves heard. Do not be like them; your Father knows what you need before you ask him.' (Matthew 6:7–9)

Father, thank you for hearing my prayer before I have even made it.

Of Course I Want to Heal You!

I remember the first time I read a book about healing, it was quite a revelation. I've never really had any ill health in my life apart from things like colds and sore throats; I've never spent a night in hospital. So I thought healing was not for the likes of me, it was for people in wheelchairs and the handicapped. It had never occurred to me that we all have very deep scars in our memories and emotions that *can* be healed!

Although I had already become a believer in Christ some time before, I didn't know how to get rid of those old habits and hangups that were preventing me from being able to live the Christian life I really wanted. I read in this book how many people have been emotionally handicapped, sometimes even with physical symptoms, because of past hurts or even unforgiveness. I recognised myself in the pages, as I knew I had carried many resentments and hurts throughout my life that originated in my childhood, and I began to have hope for the first time that I could actually be released from them.

I suddenly became aware of a new sin in my life – the sin of unforgiveness, and I wanted to immediately confess it. I went straight to Westminster Cathedral, where I knew priests heard confessions all day, and I told the priest about the book, and that I wanted to confess unforgiveness. I don't think the poor man knew what I was talking about! He was probably used to people saying, 'Father, I swore this week, and I told lies . . .', but I'm afraid the resentments of a lifetime were a bit too much for him!

Looking back though, I think the first stage of healing was my awareness of the real root cause of the problems, and the belief I could be forgiven and healed of them. Those who went to Jesus for healing showed a great faith that he could cure them, and he usually began by forgiving their sins before healing them of their problems. In the case of one man who had been ill for 38 years, Jesus asked, 'Do you want to get well again?' (John 5:7), and another time a leper told Jesus he could cure him if he wanted to. Jesus replied, 'Of course I want to', and that is exactly what he would say to us if we asked.

So first of all ask yourself what extra baggage you're carrying that burdens you – hurts, regrets, resentments, unforgiveness. Ask yourself if you really want to be healed of them, and then ask Jesus to heal you because of course he wants to!

A leper came to him pleading on his knees: 'If you want to', he said, 'you can cure me.' Feeling sorry for him, Jesus stretched out his hand and touched him. 'Of course I want to!' he said. 'Be cured!' And the leprosy left him at once and he was cured. (Mark 1:40–3)

Lord Jesus, I know you want to heal me, but help me want to be healed myself.

The RUC

I was playing a couple of concerts in Bangor, Northern Ireland, and on the first night, I found myself being brought home in a squad car by three armed policemen from the RUC! We usually only hear about them in news stories of terrorism, or allegations of their corruption or brutality towards the Northern Irish people, but my experience of them couldn't have been more different.

It was a pleasant evening after the concert, about 1.30a.m. and having earlier seen plenty of people hanging round the streets, and taxis waiting, I thought it would be nice to walk a little, and then take a taxi back to the place I was staying. I didn't realise that you can't usually hail a taxi in the streets of Northern Ireland as you might in London, and particularly after all the clubs, pubs, discos and shops had closed, everyone was waiting for taxis. I was eventually directed to a cab office where they told me there would be a half hour wait. The next cab office I tried said it would be even longer.

I was tired, slightly apprehensive about being a foreigner alone in a strange place, and I prayed for a miracle as I resigned myself to a long wait leaning against a lamppost outside the cab office! I asked God why he was doing this to me – I had to get up early to sing in a church the next morning, and I'd just played a concert to his glory. It was one of those times I was praying, not really expecting to be heard, as in my heart of hearts, I didn't see why I shouldn't have to wait just like everybody else.

Next thing, a policeman came towards me smiling and asked my name – did I really look so different to the locals? He said he thought he recognised me, as he had looked in on the concert earlier. When I explained my predicament, he said I could walk it, and I followed him for directions. To my surprise, he took me in the car with two other policemen right to the door of my destination, so they proved most unlikely angels of mercy!

While I was chatting politely to the policemen in the car, it occurred to me that these men could have been among those who had mistreated the locals. In another situation, they might be aggressive or violent, yet here they were perfect gentlemen. The men who mistreated Christ might have been like them – kind in one situation, and aggressive in another. They were just human like the rest of us, and we cannot judge all by one incident or individual. Let's remember the soldier who showed greater faith in Christ's healing power than any in Israel, or the soldier at the foot of the cross who said, 'Indeed this was the Son of God.'

When Jesus heard this he was astonished and said to those following him, 'I tell you solemnly, nowhere in Israel have I found faith like this.' (Matthew 8–10)

Lord, help me to think the best of people.

Who Owns Your Soul?

I saw a Cliff Richard video in which he was being grilled by teenagers. Inevitably most questions focused upon his Christian faith – how he reconciled being a millionaire with it and so on. Many times he would refer to God and Jesus without causing any surprise – that was of course expected in the programme. After some time though, he brought someone into the conversation who was not invited – the Devil. The teenagers probably thought, 'Now he's gone too far – nobody in this day and age can really be expected to believe in a little red man with horns and a pitchfork!' But that's precisely the problem – few people today think God is an old man with a long white beard, but the cartoon image of the Devil has survived.

Perhaps it is that we're too frightened to really believe in Satan so we find security in changing him into a harmless object of fun. Some of the newer cults which call themselves Christian are happy to accept the idea of God, Jesus and Heaven, but deny the existence of the Devil or Hell. Children often associate the Devil with the dark, and being frightened – as though he is like some bogey man from fairy tales – a witch, or a troll who will carry you off. Movies about exorcisms and other horrors also suggest the forces of evil can take you over against your will.

Well, it's taken me a lot of years, but I can finally say I am not afraid of the Devil anymore. I have now come to realise that if you give your will to Jesus, the Devil has no power over you. It doesn't mean I can no longer be tempted by him to sin; we cannot help but be influenced by the Devil, as his influence is all around us in subtle and dangerous ways. But he cannot own my will, and so with my dying breath, when it really matters, I will be able to say, 'Jesus, I want to be with you.'

The Devil can only hold power over you if you give it to him. If you live a lifestyle which belongs to him, if you dabble in occultism, or hang out in bad environments; if you surround yourself with friends who live a negative lifestyle, perhaps you will be in danger. But if you try to do what is right, even though you may fail, then Jesus will accept you as you are, just so long as you give your will to him.

> 'Yes, it is my Father's will that whoever sees the Son and believes in him shall have eternal life, and that I shall raise him up on the last day.' (John 6:40)

Lord Jesus, keep me close to you.

Justify Yourself

I was at a meeting where the leader asked, 'If you appeared before God right now, how would you justify yourself?' Well, I began to weigh up my achievements, and think of my successes in life, but before very long I began to feel they didn't really add up to much. It has been my experience in life that no matter how famous you may become, there are always people who haven't heard of you, and even those who are fans soon get over it, and we're all easily forgotten.

I can remember having been on *Top of the Pops*, and sitting in a doctor's waiting room – some teenagers were whispering about what was the name of my band, but to everyone else, I was just another patient – they didn't all watch *Top of the Pops*! Another time, some schoolchildren were crowding round for autographs near the National Film Theatre and their teacher asked, 'Who is it – Duncan Goodhew the swimmer?' I even once met a priest who had heard of neither Boy George nor *Star Trek*!

No human achievement can last all that long, and compared to all the things happening around the world each day, and the life or death decisions some people have to make, the small things

that I have been proud of in my life seemed rather insignificant. So before long I realised that it would be no good saying to God that I had had records in the charts, or I gave concerts to thousands of people, or even that I organised prayer meetings and gave witness to many. Finally, the one thing that I could offer as my justification was the same choice open to anyone else, however unknown they may be, and however unimportant in the eyes of the world – that I believed in Jesus.

I had only just arrived at that conclusion when the leader said, 'If you tried to justify yourself by what you've done, then you made a mistake – the only justification before God can be the sacrifice of Jesus.'

> Jesus said 'I am the Way, the Truth and the Life. No one can come to the Father except through me. If you know me, you know my Father too.' (John 14:6–7)

How can I thank you, Jesus, for showing me the way?

Temptation of Christ

Isn't it funny how we can go to church week after week, hear the word of God being read from the Bible, and still fail to relate it to our own lives? One evening I found myself talking about the Devil's temptation of Christ in the wilderness, and realised I had always thought that story had nothing much to do with me, but related only to Christ, and his divine powers. I have never been starving, so the temptation to turn stones into bread meant nothing to me. But I have often wanted things I could not have – more possessions, more money perhaps; I have lusted and wanted the chance to satisfy my sexual desires, and wouldn't have minded those stones turning into the object of my desires. Maybe the stones do relate to my life.

Being offered the kingdoms of the world in return for worshipping the Devil seemed a temptation for Jesus only: I am not likely to ever be offered such power, and I certainly would not worship the Devil. I should have seen though, as someone who has given concerts to thousands upon thousands around the world, I very much enjoyed the power of being their idol; I liked being on television, and was often consumed with ambition and a desire for the things the world values. Perhaps I was not really so far away from worshipping the Devil.

Finally, the idea of Jesus throwing himself from a tower to be rescued by angels was definitely not intended for me. But isn't that one about our faith? Jesus said with faith the size of a mustard seed we could move mountains, yet we're constantly putting God to the test, and doubting his ability to rescue us – well, I know I am anyway! If we could only believe God is taking care of us without having to constantly make our own plans, maybe we could withstand the temptations of the Devil rather better, as Jesus did. I certainly intend to look rather more closely at those three temptations in my own life in future.

Then Jesus replied, 'Be off, Satan! For scripture says: You must worship the Lord your God, and serve him alone.' Then the devil left him, and the angels appeared and looked after him. (Matthew 4:10–11)

Lord, help me not to want so much the things of this world, but find my rest in you.

Seen the Light

It may be a typical human tendency, but we all seem to have longings for things we don't have, and in some cases can never have – it might be a particular gift like a singing voice, or to be taller, shorter, thinner or whatever. At the same time, things we do have are often taken for granted, even though they may be gifts other people long for. If you suddenly lost your eyesight or hearing, you might remember how beautiful things looked or sounded before, but otherwise we don't stop to think what a gift sight or hearing may be – to those of us who have them, they're just *normal*!

It can be the same with relationships. We might stop and spend time in the street talking to someone we hardly know, and then not bother to say a word to those we live with. That doesn't only apply to family life, I've found in my own house, people I used to spend a lot of time with as visitors become in a funny way more distant if they become residents. I wonder if many of us who are brought up in 'Christian' homes, have the same problem with God – we can take God for granted in the same way. If we have always had people who believed in God around us, and have been taught about Christ and the Bible in school, it seems nothing special at all. On the other hand, if God suddenly became absent from our lives, perhaps we would notice the difference.

Why did shepherds leave their watch on the night Christ first came into the world? Why did wise men travel from foreign countries following a star? Although we know the stories well, doesn't it seem extraordinary that people would go to so much trouble to worship a new king? Well, Isaiah prophesied, 'The people that walked in darkness has seen a great light'. Perhaps for some of those who lived before Christ life seemed like darkness, and so the moment his light shone into the world, they could not fail to respond and go to worship him.

Yet we, who have the full benefit of his glory, seem unmoved. It may be that we each need to imagine just for a moment what our lives would be like if there was no God, no Christ, and we were all alone in the world. We might then find a new desire to worship him – to thank God for all he has done for us.

> The people that walked in darkness has seen a great light;
> on those who live in a land of deep shadow a light has shone.
> You have made their gladness greater, you have made their
> joy increase. (Isaiah 9:1–2)

Lord God, help me appreciate your light shining upon me.

Fifteen More Prayers

To complement my

album, Look at Christ,

and the Rosary

I Will Never Forget You

There was a council estate in an inner city; one of those 'no-go' areas full of tower blocks. The lifts and phone boxes were nearly all vandalised, and the walls were covered in graffitti. The stair wells, and the lifts which actually worked, smelt badly of alcohol and urine.

A young teenage girl lived in one of those blocks. She was thirteen, going on fourteen, and her name was Mary. Nearly everyone she knew was out of work; most of the families living nearby had no father; girls were bringing up children on their own, living on Social Security, and even in her class at school, some girls had had to leave because they were pregnant. There seemed no prospect of anything ever getting better: it was as though the rest of society couldn't care less. The government and the council were uninterested in those living on the estate, and most 'decent people' wouldn't even go near them. What were this girl's prospects? To leave school at sixteen with no hope of finding a job, perhaps become pregnant before long, and spend the rest of her life trying to bring up kids on Social Security? Despite all of this, Mary carried on, hoping that God hadn't forgotten her people too. But then perhaps he was too busy; perhaps he was like everyone else, and didn't have time for them.

Well, another teenager called Mary was once in a similar position. She lived nearly two thousand years ago in a place God seemed to have forgotten, where the government didn't care about them either. But God sent her a messenger to say, 'Do not be afraid . . . God is pleased with you'. The messenger went on to say that God had chosen her out of everyone who would ever live to help save the whole human race. She must have been ecstatic; even if everyone else had forgotten her, God certainly had not!

So just in case you ever feel a little bit like the two Marys in this story, remember that God is not influenced by the attitudes of everyone else; he doesn't see things as we do, or judge who is important by the standards of society. Even if you are forgotten by the whole world, he will never forget you.

> In the sixth month the angel Gabriel was sent by God to a town in Galilee called Nazareth, to a virgin betrothed to a man named Joseph, of the House of David; and the virgin's name was Mary. He went in and said to her, 'Rejoice, so highly favoured! The Lord is with you.' (Luke 1:26–9)

Lord, let it be done to me according to your will.

My Guitar

Some years ago I went with a youth group on a day retreat in Kent. On the coach they were all listening to music, and one boy had a tape of U2 blaring all the way. He later told me he played bass guitar, but was surprised when I asked him if he ever played in church – he didn't think the two things went together.

During the following week I returned to their local church, and took my electric guitar, saying: 'The focus of our prayer tonight will be this guitar. It has never been in church before, because I thought it had nothing to do with God, but now I see it has everything to do with him.

'It was specially made for me out of plastic mirror 10 years ago, before I had achieved any kind of fame. It's one of a kind, bright and shiny, and couldn't fail to be noticed! In short, it was all the things I was aspiring to achieve, and thought I would find in the world of pop music.

'My aspirations haven't changed, but now I realise the things I needed could only be found in God. My guitar used to magnify a spotlight into the audience from the stage, but now, I rather hope my soul magnifies the Lord!'

> And Mary said: 'My soul proclaims the greatness of the Lord and my spirit exults in God my saviour; because he has looked upon his lowly handmaid. Yes, from this day forward

all generations will call me blessed, for the Almighty has done great things for me.' (Luke 1:46–9)

Lord, I pray that others will see you in me.

Just As You Are

Do you ever feel a bit of an outcast, or that others don't appreciate you? Like, if anyone has to be left out or forgotten, it will be you; like, others always win competitions, but never you; like, all the good luck and great opportunities have to go to someone else?

Well, Jesus usually chose the outcasts and the forgotten, those passed over by other people.

It was not only as a man that he chose the sinners and tax collectors to mix with. On that historic moment when God came into the world as a baby, who were the first called to see the great event and to worship him? It was not the important men, the politicians or the famous; not the rulers, or even the kings – it was simple working people. In fact they were probably rather less than ordinary workers, as when all 'decent' working people were in bed asleep, these men were outside the town looking after other people's sheep. They may have been unable to get any other work because they were foreigners or in some other way considered unsuitable to be seen around during the daylight. They might have been shy or antisocial, and preferred the animals at night to people during the day!

When the glory of the angels disturbed their peace, they must have been totally shocked, in a way perhaps even the scribes and pharisees would never be, later on in the life of Christ. 'Are you sure you've got the right people?' they may have thought . . . 'Nobody's ever before chosen to bring good news to us first.' They may have even needed some convincing – can you imagine going to tell a bunch of nightshift workers in a factory to leave what they're doing, and come and worship God?

Even once they were convinced, they must have asked what they could possibly bring as gifts to a new king. Well, the message of Christ throughout his life would say, 'You don't have to bring anything; just bring yourselves, and that will be quite enough.' That message holds true for us today. We don't have to impress God with anything we can buy, bring, or offer – he just wants us as we are. Even if everyone else passes us over, he has not chosen them before us, and we will all get an equal chance to see the glory of God.

> 'Happy the eyes that see what you see, for I tell you that many prophets and kings wanted to see what you see, and never saw it; to hear what you hear, and never heard it.' (Luke 10:23–4)

Thank you, Lord, for not overlooking me.

The Right Channel

Years ago I can remember writing to my older sister in Canada to say I was nearly twenty-one and hadn't made it as a pop star yet. She advised me that we should not set limits on ourselves. One friend of mine when approaching nineteen, began to feel his youth was slipping away, and wanted to relive those irresponsible times when he was fourteen. Almost whatever age we are, the feeling of growing old may come to us. I remember once reading that it has its compensations, because as we grow lines on our faces, and perhaps become less physically fit, we gain wisdom from our experiences. That wisdom, however, may occasionally appear like foolishness to the less wise.

The Bible is full of wise old men who appeared foolish: in the Old Testament, Abraham believed he would be the father of nations even when his wife laughed at the idea of having a child in her old age; Noah was laughed at for building the ark when there was no sign of rain; in the New Testament, Simeon went into the Temple every day believing he would not die without seeing God's promised Saviour. How did he recognise the Saviour from all the other babies? How is it they all heard God speaking to them, when we may feel we never hear from God? Is God less powerful than he used to be? Has he grown tired over the years?

Well, I suspect it's none of those reasons, but rather that the wise old men of the Bible were tuned to the right channel. Our radios may be tuned to Radio One, or some more hip station, and our TVs to the latest soap, so is it any surprise we don't hear the voice of God?

Prompted by the Spirit he came to the Temple; and when the parents brought in the child Jesus to do for him what the Law required, he took him into his arms and blessed God; and he said: 'Now, Master, you can let your servant go in peace, just as you promised; because my eyes have seen the salvation.' (Luke 2:27–30)

Lord, help me tune in to your channel.

The Girl in Jeans

On a visit to Northern Ireland, one girl at a Methodist youth club asked me whether I thought her mother was being unreasonable to object to her wearing jeans to church. I suggested that perhaps the argument went deeper than what she wore, and could be more about communication between the two as she was now growing up. Maybe if she let her mother a bit more into her life and secrets, the mother would understand why the jeans were so important to her. At the same time, as the girl was now becoming a young adult, perhaps she could begin to try and understand her mother's point of view.

When all is said and done, I doubt that God cares at all what you wear on the outside – he's rather more concerned with what's in your heart, but the girl had to weigh up whether or not a pair of jeans was really worth falling out with her mother over.

Even Jesus at the age of twelve seemed to rebel against his parents. He disappeared for three days when they went to Jerusalem. Interesting, they didn't even notice him missing for a whole day – I wonder how long it takes us to notice if we lose sight of him? Why did it take them three days to find him? If you lost your young brother or child, I expect church is the last place you would look, and maybe the temple was the last place Mary and Joseph thought of looking for their twelve-year-old. His mother could not understand why he had done this to them, but he was also surprised they didn't understand.

So many family arguments are caused because parent and child each feel the other doesn't respect them, and often they don't even listen to the other's point of view. On the verge of adolescence we are all filled with questions, but too often we don't know where to turn – parents and teachers may seem unsympathetic, and our friends aren't much help when they're going through the same thing. According to the Bible, the boy Jesus spent his three days listening and asking questions. If we could only listen as this twelve-year-old did, then our Father might get the chance to give us the answers we need.

> They were overcome when they saw him, and his mother said to him, 'My child, why have you done this to us? See how worried your father and I have been, looking for you.' 'Why were you looking for me?' he replied. 'Did you not know that I must be busy with my Father's affairs?' But they did not understand what he meant. (Luke 2:48–50)

Father, help me to listen to you.

Calling You

How do you think God feels about you right now? Is he pleased with you, is he ashamed of you, do you feel ashamed when you think he knows everything you have thought and done? Well, it is hard to believe that even though he knows every single time we've let him down, he still loves us and invites us to be with him.

When Jesus had to get through his last night before suffering and dying, he invited his friends to spend the time with him. He knew all the arguments they had had in the past, he had just predicted they would all betray him and run away in his time of trial, and yet he still invited them to join him. He was fully aware that they would be of no use or support to him, and so it was not for his benefit, but for *theirs* that he invited them to 'Stay here with me and pray'. Each time they fell asleep, he again gave them the chance to support him, even though he knew his only real help could come from God the Father.

Jesus could have chosen anyone in the world as his friends, the rich, the powerful, the influential, but he chose the weak and the ordinary. That should tell us we have nothing to live up to; we do not have to become super-beings, or try to be perfect before we can approach him. He loves you and I just as we are, for all our imperfections and failings, and even though he knows every one of our arguments, and our betrayals, he still invites us to be with him, as his friends. We should never fear to turn to God on account of our sins: he could choose anyone in the world, but he is calling you!

> They came to a small estate called Gethsemane, and Jesus said to his disciples, 'Stay here while I pray'. Then he took Peter and James and John with him. And a sudden fear came over him and great distress. And he said to them, 'My soul is sorrowful to the point of death. Wait here and keep awake.' (Mark 14:32-5)

Lord, help me stay awake to your call.

Accusations

I don't know if you're like me, but if someone accuses me of something, I tend to be very quick to rush to my own defence. If someone says an untrue thing about me, I'm even more indignant, and may go to great lengths to explain every aspect of the situation by way of justification.

Something I heard a priest say got me thinking about one aspect of Christ's suffering to which I had never before given a second thought. When the priests, the servants, Pilate and Herod all accused him, he made no reply at all. I had always thought the obvious, that he didn't reply because he was not guilty, and they would not accept that. But maybe if he had replied, his answer would have been to accept their accusations as true.

They shouted all kinds of accusations at him: 'liar, cheat, false prophet, drunkard, fornicator. . .' Why did he not deny those things? Because those were exactly the sins he was dying for; if I have ever lied, then he accepted the title 'liar' for me; if I have ever cheated at anything, then he accepted the name 'cheat' for me; if I have ever indulged in sexual sin, then he accepted the insult 'fornicator' for my sin.

76

I know we have all heard this many times before, but in the light of the above, consider once again: *he died not for anything he had done, but for what we have done, and continue to do.* Bearing this in mind, I hope the next time someone accuses me of something I didn't do or say, I will just be that little bit slower in rushing to my own defence, to remind me that Christ did not deny guilt for all those wrong things – the things I have indeed done, but never been found out, or accused of.

> He had not done anything wrong, and there had been no perjury in his mouth. He was insulted and did not retaliate with insults; when he was tortured he made no threats but he put his trust in the righteous judge. He was bearing our faults in his own body on the cross, so that we might die to our faults and live for holiness; through his wounds you have been healed. (1 Peter: 22–4)

Lord Jesus, help me know when to keep my mouth shut.

Do You Remember?

Do you remember your first day at school? I can remember sitting quite contented, with paper and crayons, surrounded by kids crying their eyes out! I liked drawing pictures, so I was quite happy, and couldn't understand why all the other kids were so upset – I suppose I wasn't attached to my mother like they were. It's funny how we can vividly remember significant events like that from our early childhood, isn't it?

I don't remember a great deal else from primary school days, but one event I do remember, was also perhaps on my first school day. I stood nervously at the playground's edge at playtime (I was not used to other children, as there were none on the street where I grew up), and a boy running past spat in my face and laughed for no reason. I doubt the boy in question would even remember it himself, but clearly it made a deep impression upon me. Perhaps it has even been one of the things that influenced my strong feelings in later life about injustice.

When Jesus was arrested, they spat in his face. They also beat him, falsely accused and insulted him. When he was finally condemned, it didn't end there, as the soldiers still had to have their fun, but were they particularly cruel? Maybe one had had an argument with his wife that day; another had been passed over for promotion; another got out the wrong side of the bed – and so it continues . . .

It could be that one of them had been spat upon in a Roman playground, or made to feel inferior because of his build, his family, his wealth, or lack of it. You probably have your own memories of times you were hurt, mistreated or humiliated at school, we all do, but how has that affected the way you treat other people? You can either go through life mistreating others as you feel you have been mistreated yourself and setting into motion a further negative chain reaction, or you can treat others as you wish you were treated yourself.

> The soldiers led him away to the inner part of the palace, that is, the Praetorium, and called the whole cohort together. They dressed him up in purple, twisted some thorns into a crown and put it on him. And they began saluting him, 'Hail, King of the Jews!' They struck his head with a reed and spat on him; and they went down on their knees to do him homage. (Mark 15:16–20)

Lord, help me forgive those who have hurt me.

The Entertainer

When appearing as a guest at one of those big missions with an American evangelist, I was asked to describe the difference between what I do now, and what I did before I was a believer. I realised that in the past I was a 'performer' – an 'entertainer'. I performed like a dancing bear in a circus might, like puppets in a Punch and Judy show do, simply providing entertainment. I made all the right moves in the right places to get the maximum applause. 'Entertainment' can be comedy, it might be acting in a

play or singing, but overall the word suggests escapism – something to take people's minds off their problems for an hour or so. The difficulty is that once the show is over, when you leave, you must return to your real lives and your problems will still be there. It is also likely that the entertainment will not have helped you in any way to face up to those problems.

On Michael Jackson's 1992 world tour he appeared to 'fly' off the stage at the end of the show like Superman! One great fan of his I know who saw the show twice told me it was really like a great magic show or collection of conjuring tricks . . . in other words, it's all an illusion. The media and showbiz is full of people who wanted to be stars themselves, but failed or were not good enough, and so they keep their fantasies alive by building up the unreal images of the stars. They want you to look up to those stars so that they too might bask in some of the reflected glory. Following Jesus involves taking up a cross, but that doesn't mean we can never laugh or enjoy entertainment, quite the reverse, but we must take life as it really is, and not try to live an illusion.

I have given up being an entertainer in order to become a communicator. I know all the tricks to get an audience worked up, but I no longer use them. I have no desire to build people up into a frenzy over fantasies which have nothing to do with their real lives. Rather I wish to communicate to them that there are answers to be found in Jesus Christ.

> He called the people and his disciples to him and said, 'If anyone wants to be a follower of mine, let him renounce himself and take up his cross and follow me. For anyone who wants to save his life will lose it; but anyone who loses his life for my sake, and for the sake of the gospel, will save it.' (Mark 8:34–6)

Lord, give us the strength to live without illusions.

Sorrow

After a concert a young man came up and asked me, 'How can I be forgiven?' I said, 'You just have to ask.' How do we know that? Well, when Jesus hung naked on that tree, one of the criminals beside him said, 'We deserve to die, but this man's innocent', and in doing so he admitted his guilt. Then came the biggest shock: he said, 'Remember me, Jesus, when you come into your kingdom', to which Jesus replied, 'Today you will be with me in Paradise'. That man may have done worse things than you or I will ever do. He could have been a murderer or a rapist, but that one moment of sorrow wiped it all out . . . not in a million years, not even next year, but *today* 'you will be with me in Paradise'.

To feel the forgiveness of Christ we have to feel sorrow, but let's not confuse sorrow with grief or despair – they suggest no hope, giving up, they're totally negative feelings. But sorrow is quite different: sorrow means I've made a mistake, but I won't make that mistake again; sorrow means I may have done wrong, but it can be put right. Sorrow is a positive feeling, and in Christ, it turns hopelessness into triumph.

Despite the pitiful image in my mind of an innocent man tortured and dying in the public gaze, I can't help but feel almost joyful every time I repeat his promise. It's a promise you may want to repeat again and again – unless you're perfect; perfect people have no guilt to confess, no sorrow to feel. But if you're a sinner like me, then you might just want to remind yourself once more that if you can say in faith, 'Remember me, Jesus', then he can reply, 'You will be with me in Paradise'.

'Jesus,' he said, 'remember me when you come into your kingdom.' 'Indeed, I promise you' he replied, 'today you will be with me in Paradise.' (Luke 23:42–3)

Jesus, remember me, a sinner.

How Could it Happen?

During my pop career, I made concert tours in thirty countries around the world, from Scandinavia to the Far East, from Mexico to Eastern Europe. My vision of the world was greatly influenced by the things I saw in those places. One of the countries where we had most success was Poland, and three times during tours there, I visited Auschwitz, the most notorious World War II concentration camp. I had heard many stories about the atmosphere there, and how people could never be the same after seeing it. On arriving, it seemed to me rather like a deserted army barracks – lots of wooden huts with nothing inside; there were photos of former prisoners, but so far, no real horror – even the gas chambers had been demolished by the Nazis before they left.

After a while we came to a very large bunker with a glass front – almost the size of a small room. It was full of spectacles, shaving brushes and small personal belongings. Apparently, people thought they were going to a work camp until the war finished, and so they took little photos of their relatives, toothbrushes, etc. But in most cases, on arrival their things were taken away from them, and they were marched straight to the gas chambers, being told they would be given a shower. The next room contained a bunker full of false limbs – they would be taken off those killed in the gas chambers and given to wounded Nazi soldiers. Then came a surprise – a bunker full of human hair. Nearby was a large roll of sackcloth, and a notice saying they cut the hair from the ladies' dead bodies, and wove it into cloth. They also made lampshades from human skin, but thankfully, there are no samples on display.

I asked myself how this could have happened – why did nobody do anything? Did no one realise what was going on here? Those who lived nearby must have smelled the burning bodies, and who were the people working in the factories that made the cloth or the lampshades? Perhaps people just turned a blind eye to it; perhaps they thought they could do nothing; maybe they thought it was not their responsibility.

Pilate didn't want to face up to his responsibility either. He tried sending Jesus back to the High Priest, then to Herod, and even when he finally gave the judgement, he tried to pass the blame onto the crowd by washing his hands. How many times have you or I seen an injustice and done nothing; had the chance to give an opinion or vote, and left it up to others? The characters in the Bible are just like us, and like Pilate, we often don't want to take on our responsibilities.

But God has the power to transform any disaster into a triumph. After Jesus had been tortured and killed, just like so many concentration camp victims, and after his body had lain three days in the tomb, God brought him back to life. Polish schoolchildren are now taken to see the museum of Auschwitz, to remind them that it was built and continued in its gruesome work for many years because other people allowed it to happen. You may think this cruel, but the Poles want to be sure it will never happen again. Jesus died and rose again once and for all time, so that we would never have to die of sin again.

'I am the resurrection. If anyone believes in me, even though he dies he will live, and whoever lives and believes in me will never die.' (John 11:25–6).

Lord, may I not waste the salvation you won for me.

Empires Crumble

When the history of the twentieth century has been completed, what will be the most significant events they will record? The two World Wars; the spread of Communism; the Space Race? Recently in prayer, another picture came into my mind which I had almost forgotten, and it might well be ranked alongside those other things listed above. It was a picture of a man standing on top of a tank outside the Russian parliament building. Do you remember it now, and had you forgotten it too? It was really the day Communism crumbled in Europe, and it was demonstrated that empires can be toppled by ordinary people.

At the time, I remember thinking if all this could happen in a few short days with just people power, imagine what could be achieved together with the power of God! I wonder if the fact I forgot about it means I have become lazy, and maybe I'm not trying quite as hard to build up the Kingdom of God as those people in the USSR tried to build their ideal world?

Before Christ left his followers, he promised them special powers until his return: that they would cast out demons, speak in tongues, pick up snakes, and be unharmed by poison; that they would make the sick well again. He also promised them power from on high. If we should lose the urgency to take the Good News to all people as he instructed, then what will Christ say to us when he comes again?

He said nobody knows the hour the Son of Man will return, so could it be that when they write the history of our century, the most important event will be that Christ came back?

'These are the signs that will be associated with believers: in my name they will cast out devils; they will have the gift of tongues; they will pick up snakes in their hands, and be unharmed should they drink deadly poison; they will lay their hands on the sick, who will recover.' (Mark 16:17–18)

Lord, may I be ready when you come again.

I Hear You

On the day of Pentecost, according to the Bible, 120 believers were gathered together, terrified, in an upper room, and the Holy Spirit descended upon them all, so they threw the doors open, went out and converted 3,000 people that day. The Holy Spirit did not wait until they became perfect, or ideal Christians; most of them had run away when Jesus was captured, and they still remained cowards until that time, fearing for their own lives, and probably bickering among themselves too.

It is also assumed from the Bible account that the Holy Spirit rested upon all of them – the Spirit did not seek out the most worthy, or the most holy, but chose every single one as his resting place. So we must not assume that we have to do anything particular, or in any way make ourselves worthy for God's Spirit to come to us; the Spirit chooses the unworthy, and transforms them. The Spirit does not prefer any particular denomination or ethnic group, but is happy with anyone willing to receive him.

Once the first believers had received the Spirit, it is recorded that everyone heard them speaking in his own language. What language do you speak? You may speak the language of the pub culture, of drugs, of rock 'n' roll, but whatever it is, even if the Church does not speak to you, the Holy Spirit speaks your language!

Some people in the Church only associate the Spirit with charismatic signs – tongues, prophecy, healing – but surely speaking in everyone's language means that the Spirit can manifest in any way – to those who wish to be silent, silently; to those who prefer privacy, maybe privately, and so on. It may not be those who display how holy they are that God chooses, but those we will never hear about.

> 'It is not those who say to me, "Lord, Lord", who will enter the kingdom of heaven, but the person who does the will of my Father in heaven. When the day comes many will say to me, "Lord, Lord, did we not prophesy in your name, cast out demons in your name, work many miracles in your name?" Then I shall tell them to their faces: I have never known you.' (Matthew 7:21–3)

Spirit, breathe life in me.

Mother

One Christmas, a Christian magazine asked certain personalities for a few seasonal comments. Evangelical Christian humourist and writer Adrian Plass wrote about his personal heroine, Mary the mother of Jesus, saying she is 'usually thrown out with the bath water by twitchy, terrified protestants . . .' Another Evangelical writer has said that in Heaven, Jesus will introduce Protestants to Mary, and she will introduce Catholics to Jesus! Well, it may be true that the vast majority of Protestants seem, like Adrian Plass says, to be terrified of Mary, and many Catholics do not seem to know enough about the person of Jesus, but I'm not sure they know why they should honour Mary either! As someone who has been introduced to Mary, and then led to a much deeper knowledge of Christ as a result, I'd like to offer the following thoughts.

No Christian Church invented Mary, neither Catholic, nor Orthodox – God did! If God did not need a physical father to come into the world, then presumably he didn't need a physical mother either, but he chose one nonetheless. So for those who want to argue about Mary, your argument may have to be with God himself, rather than any particular Church or denomination. Those who claim to accept the whole Gospel cannot ignore the central role of Mary, who co-operated with God to bring Christ into the world. Since she was not a character who generally pushed herself to the front in the Gospel stories, the few times she is mentioned must teach us something. At Cana she said, 'Do whatever he tells you.' She neither told Christ what to do, nor promised them that he would work a miracle, rather she assured them whatever he said would be right. If only we could all accept his will so easily!

Many people are turned off by the sight of people appearing to worship statues, but it seems arrogant to me to think they are stupid and we know better. If their thoughts or prayers are not actually directed to the statue itself, which they obviously know is only plaster, then could it be possible their prayers are really directed to God? I cannot believe God allows any prayers to be wasted. In cultures where the mother of the family is very import-ant, often Catholic countries like Ireland, Italy, and Spain, they appear to have a much stronger devotion to Mary. Even if their own mothers have been harsh or cruel, it is rare to hear them speak against them, so perhaps the resentments in their hearts have to be in some way reconciled by turning to the mother of Jesus?

Devotion to Mary may not be essential to salvation, but God in his infinite goodness chose an earthly mother for reasons we cannot understand. Just maybe the need for us to reconcile our own experiences of what 'mother' means with his own mother, played a part.

> Seeing his mother and the disciple he loved standing near her, Jesus said to his mother, 'Woman, this is your son'. Then to the disciple he said, 'This is your mother'. And from that moment the disciple made a place for her in his home. (John 19:26–7)

Lord, help us not to condemn, but to try and understand.

Heaven

A small boy once asked a priest, 'Will there be football in heaven?' The priest asked, 'Is football essential for your happiness?' The

boy replied, 'Oh yes!' 'Well, in that case, there will be football in heaven, because you will have everything you need to be completely happy', was his answer.

Some people who believe they have died and come back to life talk about having been through a long tunnel and found a beautiful garden at the end. Personally I'm not much into gardens or gardening, so that wouldn't be my idea of heaven! Some even talk about seeing a figure beckoning, and if they are Christians, that figure may have appeared to be Jesus; if they are Buddhists, they see Buddha. Some evangelists claim visions of heaven, and have even gone into details describing musical instruments, or the surroundings. Others have claimed visions of Mary, and given great details about her hair colour, etc – interesting, though, that all these descriptions never quite agree.

Why is it that we need to look for worldly explanations and descriptions of things which are way beyond our imagining? If heaven was a place like the earth, but just a bit nicer, would it really have been worth Jesus suffering and dying so we could get there? If angels were really just people with wings, would there have been much point in God creating them in the first place? If the saints are super-beings who have achieved more than we can ever hope for, would there really be any point in trying?

No, heaven is not a place as we know places. Angels are not human beings, but spirits, and the saints are all of us who will be there in the presence of God. When you think of heaven, if you must think of a garden, or even a football pitch to give you an idea of complete happiness, then I'm sure that's fine with God, because we cannot imagine the heavenly glory of being forever in his presence.

> The Son of Man will send his angels and they will gather out of his kingdom all things that provoke offences and all who do evil, and throw them into the blazing furnace, where there will be weeping and grinding of teeth. Then the virtuous will shine like the sun in the kingdom of their Father. Listen anyone who has ears! (Matthew 13:41–3)

Lord, fill me with your glory only.